ANCIENT HEBREW
HISTORY AND CULTURE
for Kids

Ancient History for Kids
6th Grade Social Studies

In this book, we're going to talk about ancient Hebrew history. So, let's get right to it!

The Bible story of the Great Flood states that only Noah and his family were saved when God sent the floods to cover the Earth. This means that they had to populate the world a second time after Adam and Eve. The Hebrew people are descended from Noah's son, who was named Shem.

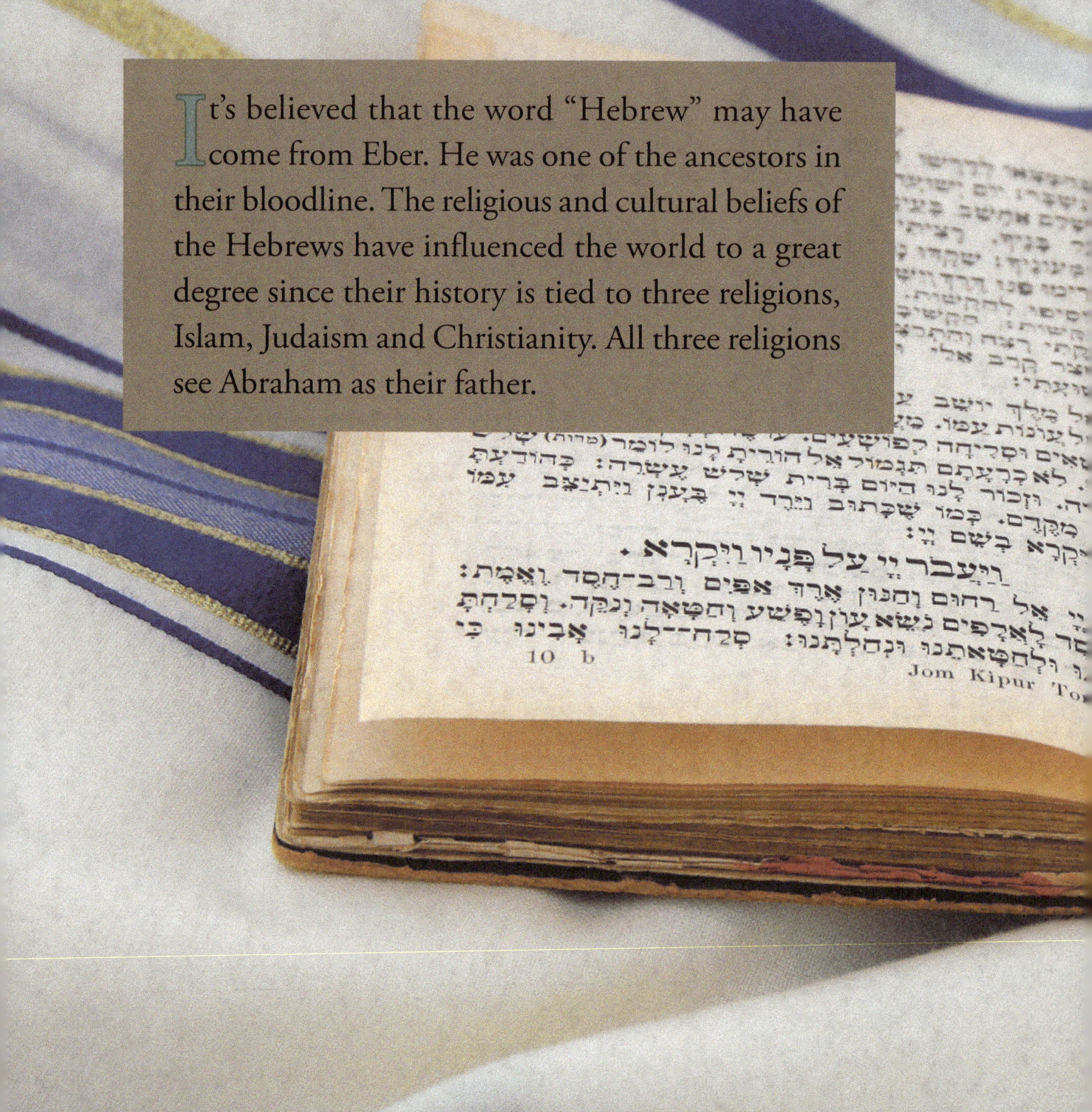

It's believed that the word "Hebrew" may have come from Eber. He was one of the ancestors in their bloodline. The religious and cultural beliefs of the Hebrews have influenced the world to a great degree since their history is tied to three religions, Islam, Judaism and Christianity. All three religions see Abraham as their father.

PRAYER SHAWL - TALLIT, JEWISH
RELIGIOUS SYMBOL.

THE BIBLICAL BATTLE AT GIBEON,
PART OF THE CONQUEST OF CANAAN.

WHERE DID THE HEBREWS LIVE?

The Hebrew people were nomads who lived in the lands we call the Middle East today. Circa 1400 BCE, they began to settle in the land called Canaan. This region was located on the eastern coastline of the Mediterranean. Eventually, Canaan was known as Israel.

After King Solomon died, the kingdom of Israel was separated into the land of Israel and the land of Judea.

Today, this same region is split into the country of Israel, as well as the countries of Jordan, Syria, and Lebanon.

KING KALAKAUA'S TORAH AND YAD

The Torah

Much of the information we have about the ancient Hebrew culture comes from the Torah. The Torah, also called the Pentateuch, was written by Moses. Scholars believe it was written originally as one volume and later divided into five different books. The word "Pentateuch" comes from the Greek language and basically means a "text in five parts." Eventually, these five books became a part of the Bible's Old Testament.

What Types Of Buildings Did The Hebrews Live In?

The land of Canaan was a desert with few trees. Wood was rare and expensive so it wasn't used for housing. The warm weather made it possible to live outdoors during most of the year. Because the Hebrews were nomadic, they often lived in tents, even when they had no plans to move. In the Torah, tents are mentioned as a common type of dwelling. Tents were inexpensive so people of lesser means often lived in tents. The people cooked and sometimes ate outdoors.

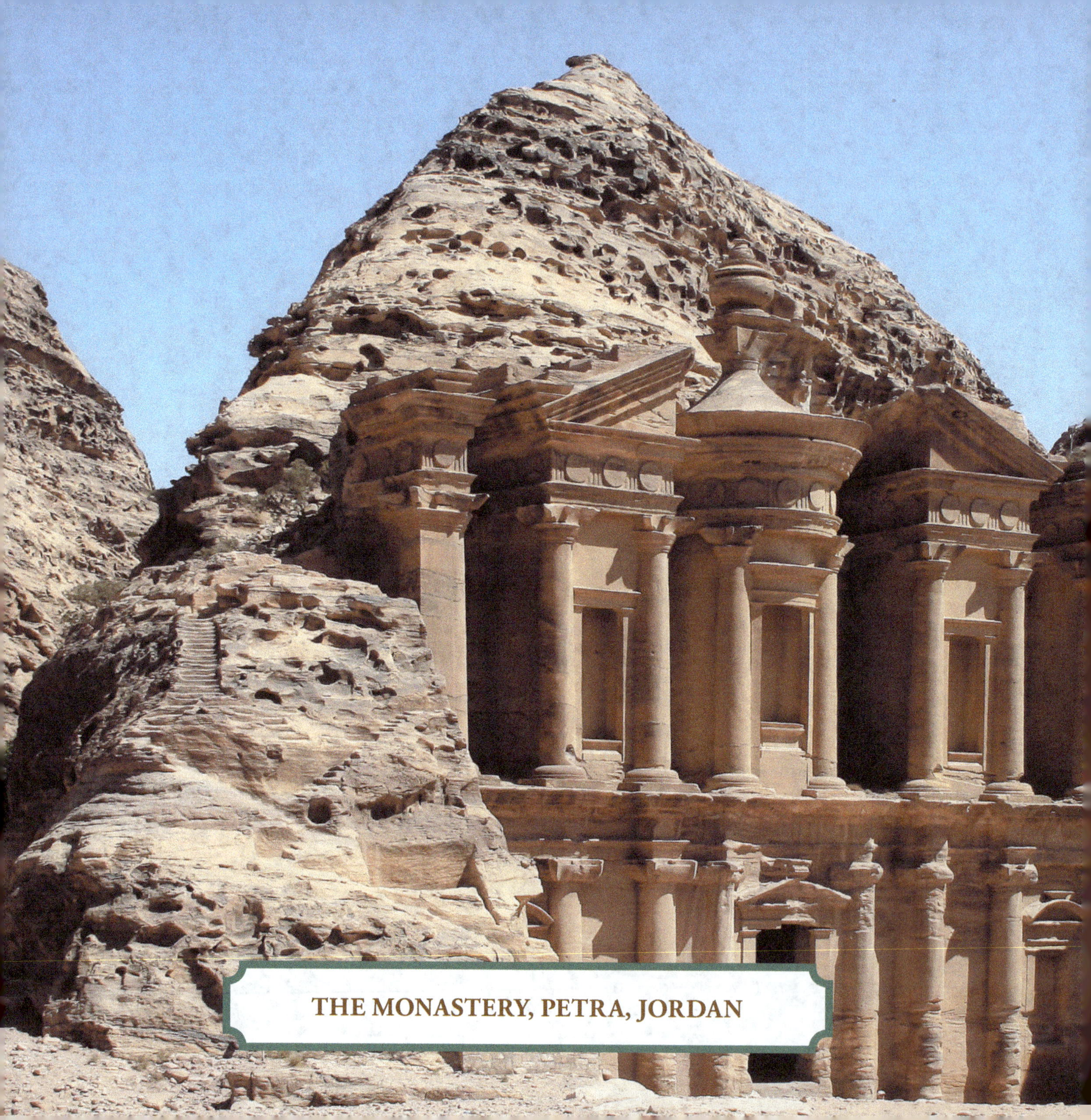

THE MONASTERY, PETRA, JORDAN

In mountainous areas, caves were sometimes used for dwellings. A natural cave was sometimes carved out further to make it larger. A wall was constructed at the entrance to convert it into a home that was secure.

The wealthy had dwellings constructed of bricks. These bricks were made of mud that had been dried in the sun to strengthen them.

The roofs of the buildings were often flat. The flat roofs offered additional space to sleep in the cool air during the hot desert summers.

COMMON HEBREW SHELTER

The houses didn't have chimneys so when someone cooked indoors, the heat escaped out the open windows. Their furnishings were very simple. They had mats to sleep on and a table with chairs where they sat for their meals. There were jugs to store the staples they used, such as grain, water, and oil.

THE HISTORY OF THE HEBREWS

The Old Testament of the Bible tells the history of the Hebrew people in stories. Archaeologists and historians have not been able to substantiate some of the history.

ILLUSTRATION FROM THE
BOOK OF GENESIS

ABRAHAM'S JOURNEY FROM UR TO CANAAN

Around 1800 BCE, Abraham, who was called "the Hebrew" in the book of Genesis, gathered the Hebrew people and led them out of Sumer. They had been living there for a period of time. They traveled to Canaan, later named Palestine.

Abraham's Descendants

Abraham heard the voice of God. It was Abraham who proclaimed that there was only one divine creator who had given life to the universe.

God told Abraham that his descendants would be as many as the stars in the sky. Abraham called God by the name Yahweh. Abraham and his wife Sarah were very old when their son Isaac was born.

JACOB, PRETENDING TO BE HIS OLDER TWIN BROTHER, ESAU TRICKED THEIR BLIND FATHER INTO BESTOWING ESAU'S RIGHTFUL BLESSING ON HIM.

Eventually, Isaac had two sons, Jacob and Esau. Jacob, later called by the name Israel, had twelve sons and they each became the head of a tribe of the nation of Israel, which was named after their father. One of Jacob's sons was named Joseph. He was Abraham's great grandson.

Joseph Gets Sold into Slavery

Joseph was Jacob's favorite son. One day he brought home a colorful coat for Joseph. His brothers were very jealous of him since their father favored him. They sold him into slavery and told their father that a wild animal had attacked Joseph and killed him.

JOSEPH IS SOLD INTO SLAVERY
BY HIS BROTHERS

JOSEPH'S BLOOD-STAINED COAT IS
BROUGHT AND SHOWN TO JACOB

They put blood on Joseph's coat and ripped it to show their father that Joseph had died. Joseph was taken by caravan to Egypt where he became a slave.

The Twelve Tribes of Israel

Joseph had the power to interpret dreams and when he began to interpret the dreams of the Pharaoh, he was released from prison and given an important job managing the resources of the Pharaoh's kingdom.

SIGNS OF 12 TRIBES OF ISRAEL

Around 1700 BCE, there was a devastating famine in Canaan. In Egypt, due to Joseph's interpretation of the Pharaoh's dream, grain had been stored up in huge quantities.

JOSEPH RECEIVES HIS FATHER
AND BROTHERS IN EGYPT

They didn't recognize their brother as he handed out the grain. At the beginning, Joseph wasn't sure that he should forgive them, but he eventually did and they came to live with him and formed the twelve tribes that were the basis for the nation of Israel.

FLAG OF ISRAEL

לא תרצח
לא תנאף
לא תגנב
לא תענה
לא תחמד

אנכי ה
לא יהיה לך
לא תשא
זכור את
כבד את

MOSES

Moses Leads Them Out of Slavery

However, during the 18th Dynasty of Egypt beginning in 1550 BCE, the Hyksos rulers who had lived in peace with the Hebrews were thrown out of Egypt. The new Pharaoh enslaved the Hebrews and they remained slaves in Egypt until Moses rose up and led them into the Sinai wilderness, around 1447 BCE.

During their time in the wilderness, Yahweh gave the Ten Commandments to Moses. The Hebrew people, now the nation called Israel, renewed their commitment to their one God and in turn God said He would bring them to the land He had promised to them.

MOSES WITH THE TABLETS OF THE LAW OF GOD

MOSES VIEWING THE PROMISED LAND

Moses Saw the Promised Land of Canaan

Moses saw Canaan, which is the ancient name for the land that was later called Palestine or Israel, before he died in 1407 BCE. The nation of Israel wasn't able to just claim the land as their own. First, they had to fight off the Canaanites who had come to Canaan from Arabia around 3000 BCE.

Finally, in 1125 BCE, there was a battle at the Hill of Megiddo. Deborah, who was a prophetess famous for her wisdom, was sent by God to go with the

Hebrew war leaders to inspire them. She was successful in helping their spirits and they were victorious. She has sometimes been described as the Hebrew Joan of Arc.

ARMY OF PHILISTINE SOLDIERS

The Philistines

Unfortunately, the Hebrew people soon had to fight another, even more dangerous, enemy. The Philistines had powerful weapons made of iron and they captured one of the most sacred objects belonging to the Hebrews.

It was the Ark of the Covenant, which was a large, gold-covered chest said to have mysterious powers. It housed the tablets that Yahweh had given to Moses with the Ten Commandments. The Hebrews lost faith that they could fight this new enemy.

ARK OF THE COVENANT

The people demanded to have a king who could rule them as a nation and go into battle for them. Despite advice from wise prophets, such as Samuel, they appointed the first king.

His name was Saul and he reigned from 1020 BCE to 1000 BCE. Saul was not successful as a king. He was soon overshadowed by a young boy named David who killed Goliath, the Philistine giant. David would soon become the new king.

King David

David grew into a mighty, as well as popular, king. He pushed the Philistines back into a thin strip of land along the coast. Under his rule, Israel became a large nation that stretched from the Euphrates River to the Aqaba Gulf.

KING DAVID

SOLOMON DECIDED A DISPUTE
BETWEEN TWO WOMEN.

He also took Jerusalem for the Israelites and recovered the Ark of the Covenant. He established a special priesthood to keep the Ark secure. His reign lasted from 1000 BCE to 961 BCE and his son, the wise king Solomon, inherited the throne. Solomon reigned from 961 BCE to 922 BCE and during this era the nation of Israel became very powerful. At the end of his reign, Solomon had turned away from Yahweh and when he died the kingdom was split in two and weakened.

SUMMARY

Although some of the dates are not substantiated, the Old Testament of the Bible tells the story of the ancient Hebrew people. The Hebrews were nomads and it was many years before they had a land to call their own. For a period of time, they were enslaved by the Egyptians, before Moses rose up to bring them to the land that Yahweh had promised them.

MOSES COMES DOWN FROM MOUNT SINAI

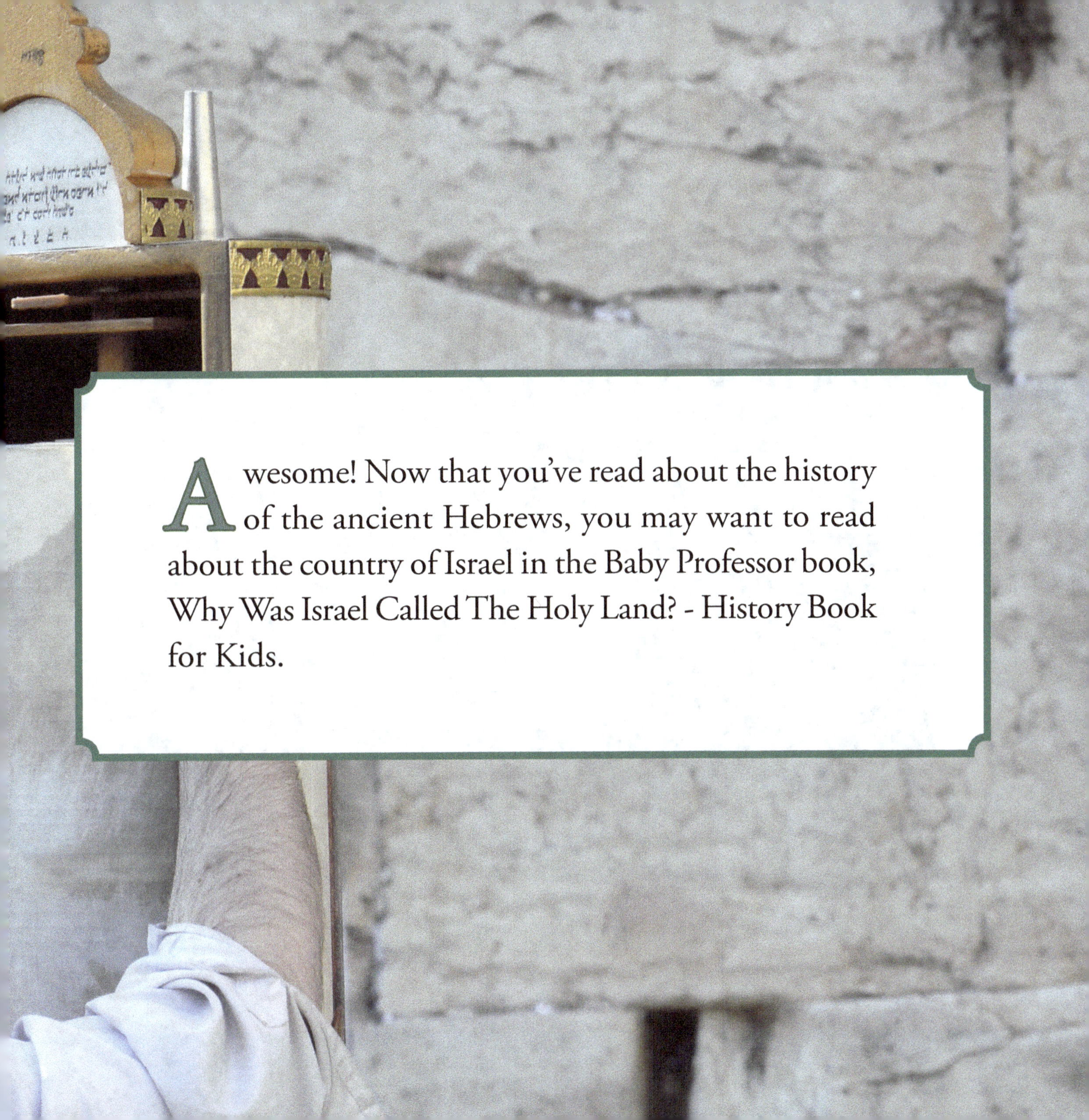

Awesome! Now that you've read about the history of the ancient Hebrews, you may want to read about the country of Israel in the Baby Professor book, Why Was Israel Called The Holy Land? - History Book for Kids.

Visit

BABY PROFESSOR
EDUCATION KIDS

www.BabyProfessorBooks.com

to download Free Baby Professor eBooks and view
our catalog of new and exciting Children's Books